REPORT

OF THE

PROVISIONAL COMMITTEE ON FOREIGN MISSIONS,

PRESENTED TO THE

General Assembly of the Presbyterian Church

IN THE

CONFEDERATE STATES OF AMERICA,

IN

AUGUSTA, GA., DECEMBER, 1861.

COLUMBIA, S. C.:
SOUTHERN GUARDIAN STEAM-POWER PRESS.
1862.

REPORT OF THE COMMITTEE.

It is well known to the General Assembly under what circumstances the undersigned assumed the responsibility of conducting the work of Foreign Missions on behalf of the Southern Presbyterian churches. The cords which formerly held Northern and Southern Christians in the bonds of harmony and fraternal love, were broken asunder, and, so far as the Southern churches were concerned, all the channels through which their united benevolence had flowed, were either very seriously obstructed or entirely cut off. In relation to the Foreign Missionary work, our people had neither the disposition nor the facilities for further coöperation with their Northern brethren. They were not unmindful, however, of their obligations to the great Head of the Church, or of the responsibilities that had been incurred upon the common faith of both sections of the Church. They were willing to sustain their full share of the common burthen; and, in the providence of God, this was assigned them, in connection with the care of the Indian Missions, and in the support of such Missionaries in the more remote field as had gone from the South. At the same time, the Indian Missions were cut off from all further connection with the Board of New York, and would have been entirely broken up, if some speedy and suitable provision had not been made for sustaining and carrying them on.

The Committee proposed nothing more than to sustain and take the control of these Missions, and also provide for the support of the Missionaries above referred to, until such time as the Church could organize and take the whole matter into her own hands.

The Address sent forth to the Churches in the early part of June has been responded to with gratifying heartiness and liberality, so that the Committee have had ample means to accomplish all that was proposed. The receipts from all sources amount to $11,145 18, being an average of something more than $2,000 per month since the issue of the Address. When the circumstances of the country are remembered, this will be regarded as very encouraging liberality, and calls for devout gratitude to Almighty God, for inspiring His people with so much interest in this great cause. A number of churches, as also individual members of the churches, have contributed more largely than they ever did before, even in the most prosperous times, showing, it is confidently believed, that the cause has taken strong hold upon the hearts of Southern Christians, and inspiring the hope that they will do still greater things when the circumstances of the country are more favorable, and when the centre of Missionary operations is brought nearer to their homes.

The disbursements have been as follows, viz:

For the support of Indian Missions,	$4,085	65
Remitted to Missionaries in Siam, China and Japan, (including cost upon exchange,)	2,224	20
Travelling expenses of J. L. Wilson to the Indian country,	180	47
Salary of J. L. Wilson, appropriated by the Committee	1,250	00
Discount on uncurrent money, cost of collecting drafts, postage, &c	31	00
Total	$7,771	12
This leaves in the Treasury a balance of	$3,373	86

The cost of the Indian Missions has been less than was anticipated when the Address to the Churches was sent forth, owing to the fact that the great body of the teachers left the country about that time, or very soon after, and there was no occasion, therefore, to provide for their support. The balance in the hands of the Treasurer will be needed for the Indian Missions at once, if the Assembly assumes the continued care of them, as no provision has been made for their support beyond the close of the present year. As yet the Committee have had no intelligence from the Missionaries in the foreign field, to whom they have made remittances, nor is it probable that there will be any for some months to come. They have no knowledge, therefore, of their circumstances, of their views of the great strife now dividing our land, or of their progress in the great work to which they have devoted their lives; and they can, therefore, lay no information before the Assembly on any of these points. It is to be presumed, however, that they are faithfully engaged in the self-denying work they have undertaken, and have, therefore, undiminished claims to our confidence, our sympathies and our prayers.

In relation to the Missionary work among the Indians, the Committee would refer the Assembly to the special report of the Commissioner who has visited them, which accompanies this, and is intended as a part of the report of the Committee.

With this brief statement, and with the report on the Indian Missions, the Committee now tender up to the General Assembly the minutes of their proceedings, the funds in their hands, and all the accounts and correspondence pertaining to the work, with expressions of sincere gratitude to Almighty God for the favor He has bestowed upon it while in their hands, and with earnest prayer that the Great Head of the Church may guide the General Assembly in all their plans and measures in relation to this great and holy enterprise.

On behalf of the Committee,

J. LEIGHTON WILSON.

REPORT ON INDIAN MISSIONS.

It will be remembered that very serious difficulties existed in the Indian territory a few months since, growing out of the national crisis through which those tribes were passing, which threatened the expulsion of our Missionary brethren there, and the complete subversion of their work; and that a Commission was appointed by the Convention at Atlanta, consisting of Rev. Charlton H. Wilson and, myself, to visit that part of the country, for the purpose of conveying the sympathies and Christian salutations of the Southern Presbyterian Church to those brethren, and of allaying, as far as possible, the excitement among the Indians, by assuring them of the interest felt by the Southern churches in those missions. We were also directed to lay the results of this visit before this General Assembly, which we now propose to do. Mr. Wilson, in consequence of sickness in his family, was prevented from complying with the appointment of the Convention. Application was subsequently made to several other brethren, well known to the churches, to take his place, but without success. I was compelled, therefore, to undertake this responsible duty without any competent adviser; but the result, I trust, realizes all that was anticipated in the appointment of the Commission. It will not be possible, however, to give the Assembly an intelligible idea of the actual state of things in the Indian country, without introducing some preliminary statements in relation to the general condition of the country, as well as the mode in which the Missionary work has heretofore been prosecuted among that people.

THE INDIAN COUNTRY—ITS SITUATION—ITS POPULATION, &c.

The South-Western Indian Territory, as it is usually termed, is situated between the States of Arkansas and Texas, being bounded on the south and west by Texas, on the east by Arkansas, and on the north by Kansas. In extent, it is nearly as large as the State of Arkansas, and for fertility of soil, abundance of water-courses, healthiness of climate, and beauty of natural scenery, it is surpassed by no portion of country west of the Mississippi. It is occupied mainly by five principal tribes of Indians, viz: the Cherokees, the Creeks, the Seminoles, the Choctaws, and the Chickasaws. Besides these, there are a number of scattered bands, as the Osages, Shawnees, Camanches, &c., to be found along the northern and western borders of the territory.

The Cherokees are the largest of all these tribes, and have a population of upwards of twenty thousand. They occupy the northern portion of the territory, that which borders on Kansas and the south-west corner of Missouri. The Creeks occupy the central portion, and have a population, it is supposed, of about fifteen thousand. The Seminoles, who speak the same language with the Creeks, occupy the western portion of their territory, but their population does not exceed five thousand or six thousand. The Choctaws and the Chickasaws occupy all the country bordering on the Red river, which separates their territory from northern Texas. The Choctaws have a population of twenty thousand, and the Chickasaws of eight thousand; both speak the same language, and in all important respects they are the same people. The entire population of the Indian territory, including the smaller bands above referred to, probably does not fall much short of one hundred thousand.

Each of the principal tribes has a Chief and Legislative Council of its own, which conduct all their civil and municipal affairs, and very much as they are done in the States. Until within a few months past, the United States Government had maintained a kind of protectorate over these tribes, settling international differences, disbursing their school funds, &c. Recently they have entered into new treaties with a Commissioner appointed by President Davis, which if ratified, as no doubt will be the case, will transfer their national relationship to the Confederate Government. It is believed that this change of relationship on the part of the Indians, with the exception of a small portion of the Creeks, is made with much heartiness. The Choctaws have already furnished one regiment for the Confederate service, and the Cherokees another, both of which are in camp, and will no doubt be found fighting shoulder to shoulder with our own soldiers in the next conflict that shall take place in that part of the country.

THE MODE IN WHICH THE MISSIONARY WORK HAS HERETOFORE BEEN CONDUCTED AMONG THE INDIANS.

The Board of Foreign Missions of the Presbyterian Church in the United States has been conducting Missions among all these tribes, except the Cherokees, for periods varying from twelve to twenty years. The work has always comprised two distinct departments of labor, viz: the educational and evangelical.

There were, until within a recent period, as many as eight boarding-schools among these different tribes, comprising in all more than five hundred pupils, and of both sexes. There were also about thirty teachers and other missionary helpers connected with these schools, the great majority of whom were from the Northern States. These schools were supported in part by funds belonging to the Indians, but disbursed by the United States Government, and in part by Missionary funds—the general rule being one-fourth from the Missionary treasury and three-fourths from the fund of the Indians. The aggregate cost of all these schools was about thirty thousand dollars per annum.

In the evangelical department there were twelve ordained Missionaries and ten native preachers and licentiates, besides a number of other native helpers. Most of these brethren, both white and native, devoted themselves to preaching the Gospel, and to the care of the churches. All of this class received their support exclusively from the Missionary treasury. Two of the native preachers, and both of them men of rare excellence and exemplary piety, have recently, in the mysterious providence of God, been removed from their work on earth to more peaceful abodes above; and three of the Missionaries, for reasons which will be assigned in the sequel, have withdrawn from their work and returned to their homes in the North.

THE RECENT EXCITEMENT—ITS CAUSE, AND THE RESULTS.

The recent excitement in the Indian country was but the extension of the same wave of popular excitement that had previously swept over every other portion of the Southern country. Vigilance committees were formed here, as everywhere else, and here, as elsewhere, undue authority was sometimes exercised by these committees. During the period of greatest excitement, all of the teachers, except three lay-superintendents of schools, left the country and returned to the

North. Some, because the term of service for which they engaged had expired; others, because there was no prospect that the schools could be continued for the present; and others, because their sympathies were with the North in the great strife now agitating the country. In view of all the circumstances of the case, it is not to be regretted that these schools have been suspended, or that the teachers have left. The buildings, and all the apparatus necessary for resuming these schools, remain in the hands of the Missionaries, so that they may be recommenced without any large expenditure of money, whenever it is thought expedient to do so. At the same time, a good opportunity will be afforded for remodeling the schools, and availing ourselves of all the modifications and alterations that may be suggested by past experience.

In relation to the Missionaries, four of them withdrew from their work during the excitement. Three of these returned to their friends in the North, but the fourth, the Rev. C. C. Copeland, withdrew to Texas with his family, feeling assured that the storm would soon pass over and allow him to resume a work in which his heart was deeply interested, and to which he had devoted the best years of his life. No violence was used towards any of the Missionaries or teachers, and no threats of violence, except in two cases: in one, by a number of Texans, who had no right to interfere in the affairs of the Nation; and in the other, by a few ill-disposed Choctaws, who, there is reason to believe, have since felt heartily ashamed of what was done under circumstances of peculiar excitement. The property seized at Tallahassee, in the Creek Nation, was no doubt done under the impression that it belonged to the Board in New York, and was therefore a legitimate prize for them. It was not in my power to visit that station, but I wrote a letter to the principal Chief, informing him that this was the property of the Southern, as well as the Northern Church, and that the matter had been referred to the Confederate Government; but expressed the hope that it would be amicably settled, without the interposition of a third party, of which there is very little doubt.

INTERVIEW WITH THE MISSIONARIES—ADDRESS TO THE CHOCTAW COUNCIL—THE RESULTS.

By previous arrangement all the Missionaries and native assistants, except one, met me, on the 5th of October, at Doaksville, the capital of the Choctaw Nation. This gave me the opportunity of a free and full conference with these brethren on all matters connected with the Missionary work, and led to many important suggestions in relation to its future prosecution, but which cannot be detailed here without extending this communication to an undue length. The Choctaw Council was fortunately in session at the same time, and gave me the opportunity not only of addressing them, but most of the chief men of the nation, who were also here at that time. In that address I assured them of the great interest felt by Southern Christians in the Missionary work going on in their country, and reminded them that the Missionaries now remaining among them had given the strongest proofs, in years past, of their general sympathy with the South, and that they had perseveringly resisted all the attempts that had been made to bring them under the influence of Northern fanaticism. These statements, there is reason to know, were received in the kindest manner by the Choctaws. The day after, two of the district Chiefs waited on me, and assured me that not only were all obstacles to Mr. Copeland's return to the Nation removed, but that the Choctaws very much desired that he would do so as soon as possible. The Choctaw Council has since passed a very flattering note inviting Mr. Copeland's return. This he has since done, and the Missionaries, when I left the country, were under the impression that they would be permitted to prosecute their work in more peace and comfort than they had done for many years past.

THE MISSIONARIES ENTITLED TO THE CONFIDENCE OF THE SOUTHERN CHURCHES.

I have no hesitation in saying that the Missionary brethren now laboring in the Indian country are not only entitled to the confidence and kind feeling of Southern Christians, but to their highest respect and veneration. No set of men have passed through greater trials, or endured more hatred and obloquy in defence of those great principles of truth and justice for which we ourselves are contending with so much earnestness at the present moment. For ten consecutive years the whole moral force of the New England Church was employed to induce them to adopt their fanatical views, instead of the plain teachings of God's Word; and when all this failed, they and their families were rudely cast off, without any known means of support. And when our present troubles first broke forth, they were the first in all that region of country to cast in their lots with the South, and no doubt their prompt and decided action had much to do in giving fixedness to the purpose of the Indians themselves. But, what still more redounds to their praise, they have been devoted, earnest and persevering laborers in the Master's vineyard; some of them for periods varying from twenty to thirty-five, and others for more than forty years. Their labors, too, have been owned by the great Head of the Church, and crowned with the most cheering results. The names of Kingsbury, Byington and Wright, are intimately interwoven with the earliest missionary efforts of this country, and are destined to become historic names in the annals of the Choctaw nation. Hotchkin, Copeland, Stark, Reid, Balentine, Lilley, and Loughridge, though they entered upon the work at a later period, have labored with no less fidelity or success. There is also a noble band of native laborers, some of whom, though unknown to fame, are destined to shine brightly in the heavenly firmament.

SUCCESS OF THESE MISSIONS.

We have already alluded to this subject, but it deserves more special notice. Modern Missions nowhere can boast of greater or more important results than among the Indians, and especially among the Choctaws. Dr. Kingsbury, who is a member of the Assembly, is the father and founder of this Mission. When he first commenced his labors among them, in the year 1818, he found them in the lowest depths of barbarism. They had not acquired the first rudiments of civilized life. Evidences of the grossest idolatry and superstition were to be seen on every hand. Intemperance, to the extent of their ability to procure the means of intoxication, was the universal habit among men, women and children. There was not a single individual in the whole nation, except two or three mixed bloods, that could read, and the only professor of religion, was the old African, Lester, who still survives, and maintains a good character for piety. But what a change has come over this people! Go among them now, in their far-off Western homes, and you will find the humblest among them living in decent and comfortable log cabins; not a trace of their former idolatry will be seen; a good little farm, well stocked with pigs, cows and ponies, may be seen in connection with almost every dwelling; intemperance is little known, and the sale of ardent spirits is interdicted by law; industry and thrift may be seen in every direction. But their most marked progress is in education and religion. It is confidently asserted, by those who have the means of forming a correct judgment, that at least two-thirds of those who have attained to a suitable age are able to read and write; whilst the present church membership, to say nothing of those belonging to other branches of the Church, or of those who have gone to their rest in heaven, is about sixteen hundred; and among no people have I ever witnessed more strikings proofs of the existence of sincere, humble and consistent piety. If these are not results in which the Church may rejoice, we know of nothing on earth that may be a legitimate subject of their joy.

THE WORK NEEDS TO BE SUSTAINED.

But whatever may have been achieved by Missions among these people, much still remains to be done. It is not possible, nor is it desirable, to attempt to perpetuate the nationality of these different tribes. The tide of white population is fast gathering around their borders, and will ere long break over all opposing barriers. No treaties, no measures of prudence, and no theories of political economy, can long prevent this. What Christian philanthropy demands, in view of this inevitable result, is, that these people shall be so enlightened and elevated, that they will be taken up by the white population, and be identified with them, and not be crushed out, as is likely to be the case with the smaller tribes in Kansas and Nebraska. This process of identification is rapidly going on in the South-Western territory at the present time, and will continue to do so, just in proportion as the Indians are improved and elevated. What seems to be particularly needed at the present moment is, to reinforce the Choctaw Mission, by sending out two Missionaries to reoccupy important stations that have recently been vacated; by furnishing one additional Missionary for the Seminole, and another for the Creek Mission, and two to commence the work anew among the Cherokees. The last-mentioned tribe, the largest of all, are now very nearly without any Missionary labor whatever—the Northern Missionaries formerly laboring among them having been withdrawn or expelled from the country.

A representative from this people is on the floor of the Assembly, and will make known their wishes on this subject. Besides this, provision should be made for the support of a few small boarding-schools among these different tribes, the chief object of which will be to train native agents, into whose hands the whole work may ultimately be committed. To carry out these suggestions, it will be necessary to appoint six new Missionaries, and the same number of teachers; and to sustain the whole work, will require not less than twenty thousand dollars.

CONCLUSION.

Such are the facts connected with the history, the present condition, and the future prospects, of these Missions. They have been so arranged and presented as to give the Assembly a comprehensive view of the whole subject, and so that they may have all the information necessary to form a sound judgment in relation to what further should be done.

The Indian tribes, in the providence of God, have been thrown upon the care of the Southern Church. There is no other source to which they can now look for the blessings of education and Christianity. They have strong claims upon our aid and sympathy. We and our kindred are enjoying the fruits of a rich inheritance which was once exclusively theirs. Many wrongs and injuries have been inflicted upon them in days that are past, and the only reparation that can now be made, is to impart to them the blessings of the Gospel. They have given the strongest proof of their capacity for improvement, and their sympathies are all with us in the great conflict now agitating the land. But, what is still more important to us as a Christian people, is, that the smiles of the great Head of the Church have attended this work in a most especial manner from its first inception up to the present moment. The best interests of this people, therefore, the honor and glory of the Redeemer, as well as our own duty and obligation, bind us to this work; and, if we may judge from the cheerfulness and liberality with which it has been sustained the last six months, there is no doubt but the whole Southern Church demands that it should be carried forward.

ACTION OF THE GENERAL ASSEMBLY.

In regard to the report and minutes of the Provisional Committee, referred to them, the Committee offer as their report the following resolutions, viz:

1. *Resolved*, That three thousand copies of this report be printed, under the direction of the Executive Committee of Foreign Missions, and we earnestly recommend that it be read to all our congregations on some suitable occasion, that all our people may learn directly its important facts, and the work to which the Master calls them: and that the minutes be committed to the Executive Committee to be appointed, and entered on their book of records, as an introduction to their own minutes.

2. That the Assembly accepts, with joyful gratitude to God, the care of those Missions to our South-Western Indian tribes, the Choctaws, Chickasaws, Creeks, Seminoles, and Cherokees, thus thrown upon them by His providence; Missions whose whole history has been signalized by a degree of success attending few other modern Missions; to a people comprising near seventy thousand souls, to whom we are bound by obligations of special tenderness and strength, and whose spiritual interests must ever be dear to the Christians of this land; a people destined, ere long, to share with us the full enjoyment of the social and political blessings for which we are now struggling; and assures those people and the beloved Missionaries that have so long and successfully labored among them, of our fixed purpose, under God, to sustain and carry forward the blessed work whose foundations have been so nobly and so deeply laid. We, therefore, decidedly approve of the recommendation of this report, that six new Missionaries be sent to this field speedily, two of them to commence a new Mission among the Cherokees, and that a few small boarding-schools be established, with the special design of raising up a native agency.

3. That in the striking fact, that the same upheaving and overturning that have called us into existence as a distinct organization, and

shut us out from present access to the distant nations, has also laid thus upon our hearts and hands these interesting Missions, with their fifteen stations, their twelve ordained ministers and sixteen hundred communicants; so that, at the very moment of commencing our separate existence, we find them forming, in fact, an organic part of our body; and, also, in the gratifying promptitude with which our churches have advanced to their support; the Assembly recognizes most gratefully the clear foreshadowing of the Divine purpose to make our beloved Church an eminently missionary Church, and a heart-stirring call upon all her people to engage in this blessed work with new zeal and self-denial.

4. The Assembly further rejoices to know that there are a few of the sons of our Southern Zion who are laboring in distant lands; and approves heartily of the action of the Committee in forwarding funds for the support of the Missions in which they are engaged, trusting that the Committee to be appointed will, as soon as possible, ascertain the facts on this subject necessary to their future guidance; and take occasion hence to direct the longing eyes of the whole Church to those broad fields where Satan reigns almost undisturbed—in India, Siam, China, Japan, and especially in Africa and South America—which have peculiar claims upon us, as fields where we are soon to be called to win glorious victories for our King, if we prove faithful; and solemnly charges them that now, while in the convulsions that are shaking the earth we hear the tread of His coming footsteps to take the kingdom bought with His blood, they should be preparing to meet Him with their whole hearts and their largest offerings. We would further remind them, in this connection, that the twenty thousand dollars required in this report for the India Missions, is by no means all that the exigencies of the cause, even during the coming year, will probably demand.

5. *Finally,* The General Assembly desires distinctly and deliberately to inscribe on our Church's banner, as she now first unfurls it to the world, in immediate connection with the headships of her Lord, His last command, "Go ye into all the world, and preach the Gospel to every creature," regarding this as the great end of her organization, and obedience to it as the indispensable condition of her Lord's promised presence; and as that one great comprehensive object, a proper conception of whose vast magnitude and grandeur is the only thing which, in connection with the love of Christ, can ever sufficiently

arouse her energies and develope her resources, so as to cause her to carry on with the vigor and efficiency that true fealty to her Lord demands those other agencies necessary to her internal growth and home prosperity. The claims of this cause ought, therefore, to be kept constantly before the minds of our people, and pressed upon their consciences, and every minister owes it to his people, and to a perishing world, to give such instruction on this subject as he is able; and to this end, the monthly concert ought to be devoutly observed by every church on the first Sabbath of each month, for the purpose of missionary instruction as well as prayer, and it would be well to accompany their prayers with their offerings. To the same end, the Assembly earnestly enjoins upon all our ministers, and ruling elders and deacons, and Sabbath-School teachers, and especially upon parents, particular attention to our precious youth, in training them to feel a deep interest in this work, and not only to form habits of systematic benevolence, but to feel and respond to the claims of Jesus upon them for personal service in this field. And should a Sabbath-School paper be established, they recommend that at least one page be exclusively devoted to this subject.

ORGANIZATION OF THE COMMITTEE OF FOREIGN MISSIONS.

PREAMBLE.

Being deeply impressed with a sense of the obligation laid upon the Church by her great Head, to "go into all the world and preach the Gospel to every creature," and the consequent claims which the various Pagan, Mohammedan, Jewish, and Papal nations of the earth have upon the Church for the blessings of a pure Gospel; feeling, too, that one of the great ends of the institution of the Church was, that she might, in her collective, organized strength, impart the knowledge of salvation to all the kindreds and peoples and tongues among men; and that, so far as it has been revealed to man, there can be no salvation for the heathen without such knowledge; remembering, also, the many tokens of the Divine favor bestowed upon the efforts of Southern Christians, while laboring in connection with the Presbyterian Church of the United States, and that an important portion of that work, in the providence of God, had been laid upon their shoulders, even before they had a distinct ecclesiastical organization of their own; and in view of the further fact that God, by His providence, has for some years been removing the obstacles that have heretofore prevented the introduction of the Gospel among the great heathen nations of the earth; and has, at the same time, bestowed upon the Southern Church all the means and agents necessary for taking a large and a distinguished share in the great work of evangelizing these nations; therefore,

Resolved, 1. That this General Assembly proceed to appoint an Executive Committee, with its proper officers, to carry on this work, and that the character and functions of this Committee be composed in the following articles, as its Constitution, viz:

ART. I. This Committee shall be known as the "Executive Committee of Foreign Missions of the Presbyterian Church in the Confederate States of America." It shall consist of a Secretary, who shall be styled the Secretary of Foreign Missions, and who shall be the Committee's organ of communication with the Assembly, and with all portions of this work entrusted to this Committee; a Treasurer, and nine other members, three of whom, at least, shall be Ruling Elders or Deacons, or private members of the Church, all appointed annually by the General Assembly, and shall be directly amenable to it for the faithful and efficient discharge of the duties entrusted to its care. Vacancies occurring *ad interim*, it shall fill, if necessary.

Art. II. It shall meet once a month, or oftener, if necessary, at the call of the Chairman or Secretary. Five members may constitute a quorum for the transaction of business. It may enact by-laws for its government, the same being subject to the revisal and approval of the General Assembly.

Art. III. It shall be the duty of the Executive Committee to take the direction and control of the Foreign Missionary work, subject to such instruction as may be given by the General Assembly from time to time; to appoint Missionaries and assistant Missionaries; to designate their fields of labor and to provide for their support; to receive the reports of the Secretary and Treasurer, and to give such directions, in relation to their respective duties, as may seem necessary; to authorize all appropriations and expenditures of money, including the salaries of officers; to communicate to the churches, from time to time, such information about the Missionary work as may seem important to be known; and to lay before the General Assembly, from year to year, a full report of the whole work, and of their receipts and expenditures, together with their book of minutes, for examination.

Resolved, 2. That this Committee shall be located at Columbia, South Carolina.

EXECUTIVE COMMITTEE.

J. LEIGHTON WILSON, D. D., *Secretary.*
JAMES WOODROW, *Treasurer.*
JAMES H. THORNWELL, D. D.
GEORGE HOWE, D. D.
JOHN B. ADGER, D. D.
A. A. PORTER.
F. P. MULLALLY.
H. MULLER.
F. W. McMASTER.
C. R. BRYCE.
CHARLES S. VENABLE.

www.ingramcontent.com/pod-product-compliance
Lightning Source LLC
LaVergne TN
LVHW020637110826
845149LV00004B/1253

9781418191221